PSYCHICAL (OR MENTAL) TREATMENT

BY

SIGMUND FREUD

British Library Cataloguing-in-Publication Data
A catalogue record for this book is available from the
British Library

Contents

Sigmund Freud

Sigismund Schlomo Freud was born on 6th May 1856, in the Moravian town of Příbor, now part of the Czech Republic.

Sigmund was the eldest of eight children to Jewish Galician parents, Jacob and Amalia Freud. After Freud's father lost his business as a result of the Panic of 1857, the family were forced to move to Leipzig and then Vienna to avoid poverty. It was in Vienna that the nine-year-old Sigmund enrolled at the Leopoldstädter Kommunal-Realgymnasium before beginning his medical training at the University of Vienna in 1873, at the age of just 17. He studied a variety of subjects, including philosophy, physiology, and zoology, graduating with an MD in 1881.

The following year, Freud began his medical career in Theodor Meynert's psychiatric clinic at the Vienna General Hospital. He worked there until 1886 when he set up in private practice and began specialising in "nervous disorders". In the same year he married Merth Bernays, with whom he had 6 children between 1887 and 1895.

In the period between 1896 and 1901, Freud isolated himself from his colleagues and began work on developing the basics of his psychoanalytic theory. He published *The Interpretation of Dreams*, in 1899, to a lacklustre reception, but continued to produce works such as *The Psychopathology of Everyday Life* (1901) and *Three Essays on the Theory of Sexuality* (1905). He held a weekly meeting at his home known as the "Wednesday Psychological Society" which eventually developed into the Vienna Psycho-Analytic Society. His ideas gained momentum and by the end of the decade his methods were being used internationally by neurologists and psychiatrists.

Freud made a huge and lasting contribution to the field of psychology with many of his methods still being used in modern psychoanalysis. He inspired much discussion on the wealth of theories he produced and the reactions to his works began a century of great psychological investigation.

In 1930 Freud fled Vienna due to rise of Nazism and resided in England until his death from mouth cancer on 23rd September 1939.

PSYCHICAL (OR MENTAL) TREATMENT
(1890A)

'Psyche' is a Greek word which may be translated 'mind'. Thus 'psychical treatment' means 'mental treatment'. The term might accordingly be supposed to signify 'treatment of the pathological phenomena of mental life'. This, however, is *not* its meaning. 'Psychical treatment' denotes, rather, treatment taking its start in the mind, treatment (whether of mental or physical disorders) by measures which operate in the first instance and immediately upon the human mind.

Foremost among such measures is the use of words; and words are the essential tool of mental treatment. A layman will no doubt find it hard to understand how pathological disorders of the body and mind can be eliminated by 'mere' words. He will feel that he is being asked to believe in magic. And he will not be so very wrong, for the words which we use in our everyday speech are nothing other than watered-down magic. But we shall have to follow a roundabout path in order to explain how science sets about restoring to words a part at least of their former magical power.

It is only comparatively recently, too, that physicians with a scientific training have learnt to appreciate the value of mental treatment. And we can easily see why this was so when we reflect on the evolution of medicine during the last half-century. After a somewhat unfruitful period during which it was dependent on what was known as 'Natural Philosophy', it came under the happy influence of the natural sciences and has achieved the greatest advances alike as a science and as an art: it has shown that the organism is built up from microscopically small elements (the cells), it has learnt to understand the physics and chemistry of the various vital processes (functions), it has distinguished the visible and observable modifications which are brought about in the bodily organs by different morbid processes, and has discovered, on the other hand, the signs that reveal the operation of deep-lying morbid processes in the living body; moreover it has identified a great number of the micro-organisms which cause illness and, with the help of its newly acquired knowledge, it has reduced to a quite extraordinary degree the dangers arising from severe surgical operations. All of these advances and discoveries were related to the *physical* side of man, and it followed, as a result of an incorrect though easily understandable trend of thought, that physicians came to restrict their interest to the physical side of things and were glad to leave the mental field to be dealt with by the philosophers whom they despised.

Modern medicine, it is true, had reason enough for studying the indisputable connection between the body and the mind; but it never ceased to represent mental events as determined by physical ones and dependent on them. Thus stress was laid on the fact that intellectual functioning was conditional upon the presence of a normally developed and sufficiently nourished brain, that any disease of that organ led to disturbances of intellectual functioning, that the introduction of toxic substances into the circulation could produce certain states of mental illness, or - to descend to more trivial matters - that dreams could be modified by stimuli brought to bear upon a sleeper for experimental purposes.

The relation between body and mind (in animals no less than in human beings) is a reciprocal one; but in earlier times the other side of this relation, the effect of the mind upon the body, found little favour in the eyes of physicians. They seemed to be afraid of granting mental life any independence, for fear of that implying an abandonment of the scientific ground on which they stood.

This one-sided attitude of medicine towards the body has undergone a gradual change in the course of the last decade and a half, a change brought about directly by clinical experience. There are a large number of patients, suffering from affections of greater or less severity, whose disorders and complaints make great demands on the skill of their physicians, but in whom no visible or observable signs of a pathological process can be discovered either during their life or after their death, in spite of all the advances in the methods of investigation made by scientific medicine. One group of these patients are distinguished by the copiousness and variety of their symptoms: they are incapable of intellectual work because of headaches or inability to concentrate their attention, their eyes ache when they read, their legs become fatigued when they walk, develop dull pains or go to sleep, their digestion is disturbed by distressing sensations, by eructations or gastric spasms, they cannot defaecate without aperients, they are subject to sleeplessness, and so on. They may suffer from all these disorders simultaneously or in succession, or from only a selection of them; but in every case the illness is evidently the same. Moreover, its signs are often variable and replace one another. A patient who has hitherto been incapacitated by headaches but has had a fairly good digestion may next day enjoy a clear head but may thenceforward be unable to manage most kinds of food. Again, his sufferings may suddenly cease if there is a marked change in the circumstances of his existence. If he is travelling he may feel perfectly well and be able to enjoy the most varied diet without any ill effects, but when he gets home he may once more have to restrict himself to sour milk. In a few cases the disorder - whether it is a pain or a weakness resembling a paralysis - may suddenly pass from one side of the body to the other: it may jump from his right side to the corresponding part of the body on his left side. But in every instance it is to be observed that the symptoms are very clearly influenced by excitement, emotion, worry, etc., and also that they can disappear and give place to perfect health without leaving any traces, even if they have persisted over a long period.

Medical research has at last shown that people of this kind are not to be looked upon as suffering from a disease of the stomach or of the eyes or whatever it may be, but that it must be a question in their case of an illness of the nervous system as a whole. Examination of the brain and nerves of these patients has so far, however, revealed no perceptible changes; and, indeed, some of the features of their symptomatology prohibit any expectation that even more accurate methods of investigation could ever discover changes of a sort that would throw light upon the illness. This condition has been described as 'nervousness' (neurasthenia or hysteria) and has been characterized as a merely 'functional' disorder of the nervous system.[1] Incidentally, an exhaustive examination of the brain (after the patient's death) has been equally without results in the case of many more permanent nervous disorders, as well as in illnesses with exclusively mental symptoms, such as what are known as obsessions and delusional insanity.

[1] See Volume II, Part X, Chapter 4 [of the work, *Die Gesundheit*, in which this paper of Freud's first appeared.]

Physicians were thus faced by the problem of investigating the nature and origin of the symptoms shown by these nervous or neurotic patients. In the course of this investigation it was found that in some at least of these patients the signs of their illness originate from nothing other than *a change in the action of their minds upon their bodies* and that the immediate cause of their disorder is to be looked for in their minds. What may be the remoter causes of the disturbance which affects their minds is another question, with which we need not now concern ourselves. But medical science was here provided with an opportunity for directing its full attention to what had previously been the neglected side of the mutual relation between body and mind.

It is not until we have studied pathological phenomena that we can get an insight into normal ones. Many things which had long been known of the influence of the mind on the body were only now brought into their true perspective. The commonest, everyday example of the mind's action on the body, and one that is to be observed in everyone, is offered by what is known as the 'expression of the emotions'. A man's states of mind are manifested, almost without exception, in the tensions and relaxations of his facial muscles, in the adaptations of his eyes, in the amount of blood in the vessels of his skin, in the modifications in his vocal apparatus and in the movements of his limbs and in particular of his hands. These concomitant physical changes are for the most part of no advantage to the person concerned; on the contrary, they often stand in his way if he wishes to conceal his mental processes from other people. But they serve these other people as trustworthy indications from which his mental processes can be inferred and in which more confidence can be placed than in any simultaneous verbal expressions that may be made deliberately. If we are able to submit anyone to a more accurate examination during certain of his mental activities, we come upon further physical consequences, in the shape of changes in his heart-action, alterations in the distribution of blood in his body, and so on.

In certain mental states described as 'affects', the part played by the body is so obvious and on so large a scale that some psychologists have even adopted the view that the essence of these affects consists only in their physical manifestations. It is a matter of common knowledge that extraordinary changes occur in the facial expression, in the circulation, in the excretions and in the state of tension of the voluntary muscles under the influence of fear, of rage, of mental pain and of sexual delight. What is less well known, though equally well established, is the occurrence of other physical results of the affects which cannot be counted as their expression. Persistent affective states of a distressing or 'depressive' nature (as they are called), such as sorrow, worry or grief, reduce the state of nourishment of the whole body, cause the hair to turn white, the fat to disappear and the walls of the blood-vessels to undergo morbid changes. On the other hand, under the influence of feelings of joy, of 'happiness', we find that the whole body blossoms out and shows signs of a renewal of youth. The major affects evidently have a large bearing on the capacity to resist infectious illness; a good example of this is to be seen in the medical observation that there is a far greater liability to contract such diseases as typhus and dysentery in defeated armies than in victorious ones. The affects, moreover, - this applies almost exclusively to depressive affects - are often sufficient in themselves to bring about both diseases of the nervous system accompanied by manifest anatomical changes and also diseases of other organs. In such cases it must be assumed that the patient already had a predisposition, though hitherto an inoperative one, to the disease in question.

States of illness that are already present can be very considerably influenced by violent affects. Such changes are usually for the worse; but there is no lack of instances in which a severe shock or a sudden bereavement brings about a peculiar alteration in the tone of the organism which may have a favourable influence on some well-established pathological condition or may even bring it to an end. Finally, there can be no doubt that the duration of life can be appreciably shortened by depressive affects and that a violent shock, or a deep humiliation or disgrace, may put a sudden end to life. Strange to say, this same result may be found to follow too from the unexpected impact of a great joy.

The affects in the narrower sense are, it is true, characterized by a quite special connection with somatic processes; but, strictly speaking, all mental states, including those that we usually regard as 'processes of thought', are to some degree 'affective', and not one of them is without its physical manifestations or is incapable of modifying somatic processes. Even when a person is engaged in quietly thinking in a string of 'ideas', there are a constant series of excitations, corresponding to the content of these ideas, which are discharged into the smooth or striated muscles. These excitations can be made apparent if they are appropriately reinforced, and certain striking and, indeed, ostensibly 'supernatural' phenomena can be explained by this means. Thus, what is known as 'thought-reading' [*Gedanken erraten*] may be explained by small, involuntary muscular movements carried out by the 'medium' in the course of an experiment - when, for instance, he has to make someone discover a hidden object. The whole phenomenon might more suitably be described as 'thought-betraying' [*Gedanken verraten*].

The processes of volition and attention are also capable of exercising a profound effect on somatic processes and of playing a large part in promoting or hindering physical illnesses. A famous English physician has reported that he can succeed in producing a great variety of sensations and pains in any part of his body to which he may choose to direct his attention, and the majority of people appear to behave similarly. It is in general true that in forming a judgement of pains (which are usually regarded as physical phenomena) we must bear in mind their unmistakable dependence upon mental determinants. Laymen, who like to sum up mental influences of this kind under the name of 'imagination', are inclined to have little respect for pains that are due to imagination as contrasted with those caused by injury, illness or inflammation. But this is clearly unjust. However pains may be caused - even by imagination - they themselves are no less real and no less violent on that account.

Just as pains are produced or increased by having attention paid to them, so, too, they disappear if attention is diverted from them. This experience can always be employed as a means of soothing children; adult soldiers do not feel the pain of a wound in the feverish heat of battle; martyrs are probably quite impervious to the pain of their tortures in the over-excitement of their religious feeling and in the concentration of all their thoughts upon the heavenly reward that awaits them. It is not so easy to produce evidence of the influence of *volition* on pathological somatic processes; but it is quite possible that a determination to recover or a will to die may have an effect on the outcome even of severe and precarious illnesses.

Our interest is most particularly engaged by the mental state of *expectation*, which puts in motion a number of mental forces that have the greatest influence on the onset and cure of physical diseases. *Fearful* expectation is certainly not without its effect on the result. It would be of importance to know with certainty whether it has as great a bearing as is supposed on falling ill; for instance, whether it is true that during an epidemic those who are afraid of contracting the illness are in the greatest danger. The contrary state of mind, in which expectation is coloured by hope and faith, is an effective force with which we have to reckon, strictly speaking, in *all* our attempts at treatment and cure. We could not otherwise account for the peculiar results which we find produced by medicaments and therapeutic procedures.

The most noticeable effects of this kind of expectation coloured by faith are to be found in the 'miraculous' cures which are brought about even to-day under our own eyes without the help of any medical skill. Miraculous cures properly so-called take place in the case of believers under the influence of adjuncts calculated to intensify religious feelings - that is to say, in places where a miracle-working image is worshipped, or where a holy or divine personage has revealed himself to men and has promised them relief from their sufferings in return for their worship, or where the relics of a saint are preserved as a treasure. Religious faith alone does not seem to find it easy to suppress illness by means of expectation; for as a rule other contrivances as well are brought into play in the case of miraculous cures. The times and seasons at which divine mercy is sought must be specially indicated; the patient must submit to physical toil, to the trials and sacrifices of a pilgrimage, before he can become worthy of this divine mercy.

It would be convenient, but quite wrong, simply to refuse all credence to these miraculous cures and to seek to explain the accounts of them as a combination of pious fraud and inaccurate observation. Though an explanation of this kind may often be justified, it is not enough to enable us to dismiss entirely the fact of miraculous cures. They do really occur and have occurred at every period of history. And they concern not merely illnesses of mental origin - those, that is, which are based on 'imagination' and are therefore likely to be especially affected by the circumstances of a pilgrimage - but also illnesses with an 'organic' basis which had previously resisted all the efforts of physicians.

There is no need, however, to bring forward anything other than mental forces in order to explain miraculous cures. Even under conditions such as these, nothing happens that can be considered as beyond our understanding. Everything proceeds naturally. Indeed, the power of religious faith is reinforced in these cases by a number of eminently human motive forces. The individual's pious belief is intensified by the enthusiasm of the crowd of people in whose midst he makes his way as a rule to the sacred locality. All the mental impulses of an individual can be enormously magnified by group influence such as this. In cases in which someone proceeds to the holy place by himself, the reputation of the place and the respect in which it is held act as substitutes for the influence of the group, so that in fact the power of a group is once more in operation. And there is yet another way in which this influence makes itself felt. Since it is well known that divine mercy is always shown only to a few of the many who seek it, each of these is eager to be among the chosen few; the ambition that lies hidden in everyone comes to the help of pious faith. Where so many powerful forces converge, we need feel no surprise if the goal is sometimes really reached.

Even those who are without religious faith need not forgo miraculous cures. In their case reputation and group-influence act as a complete substitute for faith. There are always fashionable treatments and fashionable physicians, and these play an especially dominant part in high society, where the most powerful psychological motive forces are the endeavour to excel and to do what the 'best' people do. Fashionable treatments of this kind produce therapeutic results which are outside the scope of their actual power, and the same procedures effect far more in the hands of a fashionable doctor (who, for instance, may have become well-known as an attendant upon some prominent personality) than in those of another physician. Thus there are human as well as divine miracle-workers. Such men, however, who have reached eminence owing to the favour of fashion and of imitation, soon lose their power, as is to be expected from the nature of the forces which give it to them.

An intelligible dissatisfaction with the frequent inadequacy of the help afforded by medical skill, and perhaps, too, an internal rebellion against the duress of scientific thought, which reflects the remorselessness of nature, have in all periods (and in our own once more) imposed a strange condition on the therapeutic powers alike of persons and of procedures. The necessary faith only emerges if the practitioner is not a doctor, if he can boast of having no knowledge of the scientific basis of therapeutics, if the procedure has not been subjected to accurate testing but is recommended by some popular prejudice. Hence it is that we find a swarm of 'nature cures' and 'nature healers', who compete with physicians in the exercise of their profession and of whom we can at least say with some degree of certainty that they do far more harm than good. If this gives us grounds for blaming the patients' faith, we must yet not be so ungrateful as to forget that the same force is constantly at work in support of our own medical efforts. The results of every procedure laid down by the physician and of every treatment that he undertakes are probably composed of two portions. And one of these, which is sometimes greater and sometimes less, but can never be completely disregarded, is determined by the patient's mental attitude. The faith with which he meets the immediate effect of a medical procedure

16

depends on the one hand on the amount of his own desire to be cured, and on the other hand on his confidence that he has taken the right steps in that direction - of his general respect, that is, for medical skill - and, further, on the power which he attributes to his doctor's personality, and even on the purely human liking aroused in him by the doctor. There are some physicians who have a greater capacity than others for winning their patients' confidence; a patient will often feel better the very moment the doctor enters his room.

Physicians have practised mental treatment from the beginning of time, and in early days to a far greater extent even than to-day. If by mental treatment we mean an endeavour to produce such mental states and conditions in the patient as will be the most propitious for his recovery, this kind of medical treatment is historically the oldest. Psychical treatment was almost the only sort at the disposal of the peoples of antiquity, and they invariably reinforced the effects of therapeutic potions and other therapeutic measures by intensive mental treatment. Such familiar procedures as the use of magical formulas and purificatory baths, or the elicitation of oracular dreams by sleeping in the temple precincts, can only have had a curative effect by psychical means. The physician's personality acquired a reputation derived directly from divine power, since in its beginnings the art of healing lay in the hands of priests. So that then as now the physician's personality was one of the chief instruments for bringing the patient into a state of mind favourable for his recovery.

Now, too, we begin to understand the 'magic' of words. Words are the most important media by which one man seeks to bring his influence to bear on another; words are a good method of producing mental changes in the person to whom they are addressed. So that there is no longer anything puzzling in the assertion that the magic of words can remove the symptoms of illness, and especially such as are themselves founded on mental states.

All the mental influences which have proved effective in curing illnesses have something incalculable about them. Affects, concentration of the will, distracting the attention, expectation coloured by faith - all of these forces, which occasionally remove an illness, sometimes fail to do so without there being anything in the character of the illness to account for the different result. What stands in the way of regularity in the therapeutic results achieved is evidently the autocratic nature of the personalities of the subjects, with their variety of mental differences. Since physicians came to realize clearly the important part played in recovery by the patient's state of mind, the idea naturally occurred to them of no longer leaving it to the patient to decide how much mental compliance he should show but of deliberately imposing a propitious state of mind by suitable methods.

It is from this attempt that modern mental treatment has taken its start.

Quite a number of different methods of treatment have thus arisen, some of them simple to arrive at and others which could only be reached on the basis of complex hypotheses. It is easy to see, for instance, that the physician, who can no longer command respect as a priest or as the possessor of secret knowledge, should use his personality in such a way as to gain his patient's confidence and, to some degree, his affection. He himself may succeed in doing this with only a limited number of patients, whereas other patients, according to their inclinations and degree of education, will be attracted to other physicians. Such a distribution will serve a useful purpose; but *if the right of a patient to make a free choice of his doctor were suspended, an important precondition for influencing him mentally would be abolished.*

There are many very effective mental procedures which the physician is obliged to renounce. He either has not the power or has not the right to invoke them. This applies in particular to the provocation of strong affects - the most powerful of all the means by which the mind affects the body. The vicissitudes of life often cure illnesses through the experience of great joy, through the satisfaction of needs or the fulfilment of wishes. The physician, who is often impotent outside his profession, cannot compete along these lines. It might be more within his power to employ fear and fright for therapeutic ends; but, except in the case of children, he must have the gravest doubts about the use of such double-edged tools. On the other hand, the physician must rule out any relations with his patient that are bound up with tender feelings, owing to their implications in practical life. Thus from the first his power to bring about mental changes in his patients seems so restricted that mental treatment conducted on a deliberate plan would seem to offer no advantages over the earlier haphazard method.

The physician can seek to direct his patient's volition and attention, and he has good grounds for doing so in the case of various pathological conditions. He may, for instance, persistently oblige a person who believes he is paralysed to carry out the movements of which he professes himself incapable; or he may refuse to fall in with the wishes of an anxious patient who insists on being examined for an illness from which he is quite certainly not suffering. In these instances the physician will be taking the right course, but such isolated cases would scarcely justify us in setting up mental treatment as a special therapeutic procedure. There exists, nevertheless, a queer and unforeseeable method which offers the physician a possibility of exercising a profound, even though transitory, influence on the mental life of his patients and of employing that influence for therapeutic purposes.

It has long been known, though it has only been established beyond all doubt during the last few decades, that it is possible, by certain gentle means, to put people into a quite peculiar mental state very similar to sleep and on that account described as 'hypnosis'. The various means by which hypnosis can be brought about have at first sight little in common. It is possible to hypnotize someone by getting him to stare fixedly at a bright object for some minutes, or by holding a watch to his ear for a similar length of time, or by repeatedly passing the open hands, at a short distance away, over his face and limbs. But the same result can be brought about by describing the onset of the state of hypnosis and its characteristics quietly and firmly to the subject - that is, by 'talking him into' hypnosis. The two procedures may also be combined. We may make the subject sit down, hold a finger in front of his eyes, tell him to gaze at it fixedly and then say to him: 'You're feeling tired. Your eyes are closing; you can't hold them open. Your limbs are heavy; you can't move them any more. You're falling asleep---' and so on. It will be observed that all the procedures have in common a fixing of the attention; in those first mentioned the attention is fatigued by slight and monotonous sensory stimuli. It is not yet satisfactorily explained, however, how it comes about that mere talking produces exactly the same state as the other procedures. Experienced hypnotists assert that by these means a definite hypnotic change can be brought about in some eighty per cent of subjects. There is no way of telling beforehand, however, which subjects are hypnotizable and which are not. Illness is far from being one of the necessary preconditions of hypnosis: normal people are said to be particularly easy to hypnotize, while some neurotics can only be hypnotized with great difficulty and the insane are completely resistant. The hypnotic state exhibits a great variety of gradations. In its lightest degree the hypnotic subject is aware only of something like a slight insensibility, while the most extreme degree, which is marked by special peculiarities, is known as 'somnambulism', on account of its resemblance to the natural phenomenon of sleep-walking. But hypnosis is in no sense a sleep like our nocturnal sleep or like the sleep produced by drugs. Changes occur in it and mental functions are retained during it which are absent in normal sleep.

Some of the phenomena of hypnosis (for instance, alterations in muscular activity) possess a merely scientific interest. But the most significant indication of hypnosis, and the most important one from our point of view, lies in the hypnotic subject's attitude to his hypnotist. While the subject behaves to the rest of the external world as though he were asleep, that is, as though all his senses were diverted from it, he is *awake* in his relation to the person who hypnotized him; he hears and sees him alone, and him he understands and answers. This phenomenon, which is described as *rapport* in the case of hypnosis, finds a parallel in the way in which some people sleep - for instance, a mother who is nursing her baby. It is so striking that it may well lead us to an understanding of the relation between the hypnotic subject and the hypnotist.

But the fact that the subject's universe is, so to say, confined to the hypnotist is not the whole story. There is the further fact of the former's *docility* in relation to the latter: he becomes obedient and credulous - in the case of deep hypnosis, to an almost unlimited extent. And the manner in which this obedience and credulity are carried out reveals a characteristic of the hypnotic state, namely that in the hypnotized subject the influence of the mind over the body is extraordinarily increased. If the hypnotist says 'You can't move your arm', the arm drops motionless; the subject obviously tries with all his strength but is unable to move it. If the hypnotist says: 'Your arm's moving of its own accord, you can't stop it', the arm moves and the subject is seen making vain efforts to keep it still. The idea which the hypnotist has given to the subject by his words has produced in him precisely the mental-physical behaviour corresponding to the idea's content. This implies on the one hand obedience but on the other an increase in the physical influence of an idea. Words have once more regained their magic.

The same thing happens in the domain of sense perceptions. The hypnotist says: 'You see a snake; you're smelling a rose; you're listening to the loveliest music', and the hypnotic subject sees, smells and hears what is required of him by the idea that he has been given. How do we know that the subject really has these perceptions? It might be thought that he is only pretending to have them. But after all we have no reason for doubts on the point; for he behaves exactly as though he had them, he expresses all the appropriate emotions, and in some circumstances he can even describe his imaginary perceptions and experiences after the hypnosis is at an end. We then perceive that he has been seeing and hearing just as we see and hear in dreams - he has been 'hallucinating'. He was evidently so credulous in relation to the hypnotist that he was *convinced* that there must be a snake to be seen when the hypnotist told him so; and this conviction had such a strong effect on his body that he really saw the snake - a thing which, incidentally, can sometimes happen even to people who have not been hypnotized.

It may be remarked, by the way, that, outside hypnosis and in real life, credulity such as the subject has in relation to his hypnotist is shown only by a child towards his beloved parents, and that an attitude of similar subjection on the part of one person towards another has only one parallel, though a complete one - namely in certain love-relationships where there is extreme devotion. A combination of exclusive attachment and credulous obedience is in general among the characteristics of love.

Some further points may be mentioned in connection with the state of hypnosis. The words spoken by the hypnotist which have the magical results that I have described are known as a 'suggestion' and it has become customary to apply the term as well where there is merely an intention to produce a similar effect. Not only do the hypnotic subject's movements and feelings obey suggestions, but all his other mental activities; and he does not as a rule take any action on his own initiative. Hypnotic obedience can be employed in making a number of highly remarkable experiments, which afford a deep insight into the workings of the mind and produce in the observer an ineradicable conviction of the unsuspected power of the mind over the body. Just as a hypnotized subject can be obliged to see what is not there, so he can be forbidden to see what *is* there and is seeking to impress itself on his senses - some particular person, for instance. (This is known as a 'negative hallucination'.) The person in question then finds it impossible to attract the subject's attention by any kind of stimulation; he is treated as though he were 'thin air'. Again, a suggestion may be made to the subject to carry out some action a certain length of time after waking from hypnosis ('post-hypnotic suggestion'); the subject keeps to the allotted time and performs the suggested action in the middle of his waking state without being able to give any reason for it. If he is asked why he has done what he has, he will either refer to an obscure impulse which he was unable to resist, or he will invent some half-satisfactory excuse without remembering the real explanation - namely the suggestion he has been given.

The state of hypnosis is brought to an end without any difficulty by the hypnotist's authority asserted in the words: 'Wake up!' After the deepest hypnosis there is no recollection of anything that has been experienced during it under the hypnotist's influence. That portion of the subject's mental life remains cut off, as it were, from the rest. Other subjects retain a dream-like memory, and yet others remember everything but report that they have been under an irresistible mental compulsion.

The scientific gain brought to physicians and psychologists by a knowledge of the facts of hypnotism can scarcely be exaggerated. But in order to gauge the practical importance of the new discoveries we must put a physician in place of the hypnotist and a patient in place of the hypnotic subject. Hypnosis would then seem pre-ordained to fulfil all the physician's requirements, in so far as he seeks to act towards the patient as a 'mind-doctor'. Hypnosis endows the physician with an authority such as was probably never possessed by the priest or the miracle man, since it concentrates the subject's whole interest upon the figure of the physician; it does away with the autocratic power of the patient's mind which, as we have seen, interferes so capriciously with the influence of the mind over the body; it automatically produces an increase of the mind's control over the body, such as is normally to be observed only as an effect of the most powerful emotions; and, owing to the possibility of arranging that the instructions given to the patient during hypnosis shall only become manifest subsequently, in his normal state - owing, that is, to post-hypnotic suggestion -, hypnosis enables the physician to use the great power he wields during hypnosis in order to bring about changes in the patient in his waking condition. A simple pattern of procedure would thus seem to emerge for the purposes of mental treatment: the physician puts the patient into a state of hypnosis, he suggests to him (according to the particular circumstances) that he is not ill and that after waking he will not be aware of his symptoms. The physician then wakes the patient up and may feel confident that the suggestion has done its duty against the illness. And if a single application of this procedure were not sufficient, it could be repeated as many times as necessary.

There is only one consideration that might discourage the physician and the patient from making use of such a promising therapeutic method: the possibility that the advantages of hypnotism might be balanced by some damage - if, for instance, it left behind it a permanent disorder or weakness in the subject's mind. But enough experience has already been gained to set aside such doubts: single hypnotic treatments are completely harmless and even if they are frequently repeated they are on the whole without bad effects. Only one point is to be noticed: if circumstances demand a persistent use of hypnotism, the patient falls into a habit of hypnosis and dependence on the physician which cannot be among the purposes of the therapeutic procedure.

Thus hypnotic treatment really implies a great extension of medical power and consequently an advance in therapy. Every sufferer may be advised to entrust himself to it, so long as it is carried out by an experienced and trustworthy physician. Hypnosis should, however, be used in a manner different from what is usual to-day. As a rule this method of treatment is only embarked upon after every other method has failed and when the patient is already despondent and dejected. He has then to leave his own doctor, who cannot or does not employ hypnotism, and turn to a strange doctor, who as a rule does not or cannot employ anything else. Both practices are disadvantageous to the patient. The family doctor should himself be familiar with hypnotic procedure and he should make use of it from the first, as soon as he judges the illness and the patient appropriate for it. Wherever hypnotism can be employed it should be on a par with other therapeutic procedures and should not be regarded as a last resort or even as a descent from science to quackery. But hypnotism can be employed not only in all nervous conditions and in disorders due to the 'imagination', as well as for breaking morbid habits (such as alcoholism, morphine addiction, or sexual aberrations), but also in many organic diseases, even of an inflammatory nature, in which, though the underlying disorder persists, there is a prospect of relieving the symptoms (such as pains or impediments to movement) which are troubling the patient. The selection of cases for hypnotic treatment must depend entirely on the judgement of the physician.

The time has now come, however, to dissipate the notion that with the expedient of hypnosis a period of easy miracle-working has dawned for the physician. A number of circumstances must be taken into account which are calculated to lower our expectations from hypnotic therapy considerably, and to reduce to their proper proportions the hopes that may have been raised in patients. First and foremost, one of the basic assumptions turns out to be untenable: namely, that hypnosis makes it possible to deprive patients of the interfering autocratic element in their mental behaviour. In fact they retain it, and manifest it even in their attitude to the attempt to hypnotize them. It was stated above that some eighty per cent of people can be hypnotized; but that high figure is only reached by including among the positive cases any that show the slightest sign of being influenced. Really deep hypnoses, with complete tractability, such as are chosen as examples in describing the state, are actually rare or at all events not as frequent as one would wish from the therapeutic point of view. The impression made by this fact can, however, in turn be modified when it is borne in mind that depth of hypnosis and tractability to suggestions do not go *pari passu*; so that one often sees good suggestive results where there is no more than a slight hypnotic insensibility. But even if we consider hypnotic tractability independently, as being the more essential feature of the condition, it has to be admitted that different people show their idiosyncrasies by only letting themselves be influenced up to a certain degree of tractability, at which point they come to a halt. Thus different people show a very varying degree of suitability for hypnotic treatment. If it were possible to find a means by which all these various grades of the hypnotic state could be intensified to(the point of complete hypnosis, the idiosyncrasies of patients would once more have been eliminated and the ideal of mental treatment would have been attained. But this advance has not yet been made; it still depends far more on the patient than on the physician with what degree of tractability a suggestion will be received - it depends once more, that is, upon the patient's choice.

And there is another, still more important consideration. In describing the very remarkable results of suggestion, people are only too ready to forget that here, as in all mental operations, relative size and strength must be taken into account. If we put a healthy person into deep hypnosis and then tell him to take a bite out of a potato under the impression that it is a pear, or if we tell him that he is meeting one of his acquaintances and must greet him as such, he is likely to prove completely tractable, because the hypnotized subject has no serious reason for resisting the suggestion. But in the case of other instructions - if, for instance, we ask a naturally modest girl to uncover herself or if we ask an honest man to steal some valuable object - we may already find the subject putting up a resistance, which may even go to the length of his refusing to obey the suggestion. This teaches us that even in the best hypnosis suggestion does not exercise unlimited power but only power of a definite strength. The hypnotic subject will make small sacrifices, but, just as though he were awake, he hesitates before making great ones. If, then, we are dealing with a patient, and urge him by suggestion to give up his illness, we perceive that this means a great sacrifice to him and not a small one. Here the power of suggestion is contending against the force which created the symptom, and maintains them, and experience shows that that force is of quite a different order of strength from hypnotic influences. The same patient who is perfectly tractable in putting himself into any dream-situation one may suggest to him (if it is not actually objectionable) may remain completely recalcitrant towards a suggestion which denies the reality of, let us say, an imaginary paralysis. There is the further fact, moreover,

31

that precisely neurotic patients are for the most part bad hypnotic subjects, so that the struggle against the powerful forces by which the illness is rooted in the patient's mind has to be waged not by a complete hypnotic influence but only by a fragment of it.

Thus suggestion is not certain as a matter of course of defeating the illness as soon as hypnosis (even deep hypnosis) has been achieved. A further battle has to be fought, and its outcome is very often uncertain. A single hypnotic treatment will accordingly effect nothing against severe disturbances of mental origin. If, however, hypnosis is repeated, it loses some of the miraculous effect which the patient may perhaps have anticipated. A succession of hypnoses may eventually bring about by degrees the influence over the illness which was lacking at first, till in the end a satisfactory result is achieved. But a hypnotic treatment such as this may be just as tedious and wearisome as a treatment of any other kind.

There is yet another way in which the relative weakness of suggestion is betrayed as compared with the illnesses it has to combat. It is true that suggestion can bring about a cessation of the symptoms of an illness - but only for a short time. At the end of this time they return and have to be repelled once again by renewed hypnosis and suggestion. If this course of events is repeated often enough, it usually exhausts the patience both of the patient and the physician and ends in the abandonment of hypnotic treatment. These, too, are the cases in which the patient becomes dependent on the physician and a kind of addiction to hypnosis is established.

It is a good thing for patients to be aware of these weaknesses in hypnotic therapy and of the possibilities of disappointment in its use. The curative power of hypnotic suggestion is something real and it needs no exaggerated recommendation. On the other hand, it is not surprising that physicians, to whom hypnotic mental treatment promised so much more than it could give, are indefatigable in their search for other procedures, which would make possible a deeper, or at least a less unpredictable, influence on a patient's mind. It may safely be anticipated that systematic modern mental treatment, which is a quite recent revival of ancient therapeutic methods, will provide physicians with far more powerful weapons for the fight against illness. A deeper insight into the processes of mental life, the beginnings of which are based precisely on hypnotic experience, will point out the ways and means to this end.

www.ingramcontent.com/pod-product-compliance
Lightning Source LLC
Chambersburg PA
CBHW021339290326
41933CB00038B/988